YOUR KNOWLEDGE HAS VALUE

Peter Maine

Are Niche Markets Opportunities for Growth?

GRIN Verlag

Bibliografische Information der Deutschen Nationalbibliothek:

Die Deutsche Bibliothek verzeichnet diese Publikation in der Deutschen National-
bibliografie; detaillierte bibliografische Daten sind im Internet über http://dnb.d-
nb.de/ abrufbar.

Imprint:

Copyright © 2011 GRIN Verlag GmbH
Druck und Bindung: Books on Demand GmbH, Norderstedt Germany
ISBN: 978-3-656-58014-0

This book at GRIN:

http://www.grin.com/en/e-book/267609/are-niche-markets-opportunities-for-
growth

GRIN - Your knowledge has value

Der GRIN Verlag publiziert seit 1998 wissenschaftliche Arbeiten von Studenten, Hochschullehrern und anderen Akademikern als eBook und gedrucktes Buch. Die Verlagswebsite www.grin.com ist die ideale Plattform zur Veröffentlichung von Hausarbeiten, Abschlussarbeiten, wissenschaftlichen Aufsätzen, Dissertationen und Fachbüchern.

Visit us on the internet:

http://www.grin.com/

http://www.facebook.com/grincom

http://www.twitter.com/grin_com

Are Niche Markets Opportunities for Growth?

Articles Used:

1 http://ag.arizona.edu/AREC/wemc/nichemarkets/01whatarenichemarkets.pdf

2 http://ufdcimages.uflib.ufl.edu/CA/00/40/02/13/00001/PDF.pdf

3 http://sbaer.uca.edu/research/icsb/2009/paper1.pdf

Darmar pursues a Niche strategy by supplying small retail outlets with Indonesian artifacts. This is a niche market because the small retail outlets find it difficult to import the artifacts into United States from Indonesia and the artifacts also are difficult to be produced in large numbers for wholesalers. This provides Darmar with a market where there are no competitors hence the potential to supply the artifacts to small retailers. Essentially, the business is advantaged because good relationships have been established by the designers of the artifacts who are mostly people her family is close with. Darmar has it as a targeted part of the market where she understands the needs of both his customers and suppliers. This is illustrated in the ability to make the designers create what her market requires.

An article written by Wong-MingJi (1999), niche markets are not addressed in detail by the mainstream providers hence it is easy to focus on a specific client's group hence ability to satisfy them. This defines the kind of products that you offer since competition is low or unavailable. Designs are customer oriented since the needs of the customers determines what to be targeted in the market. Darmar has completely identified the needs of her customers and how difficult it is for them to successfully access the resources to use in their businesses. The larger wholesalers find it difficult to mobilize the Indonesians to achieve mass production of the artifacts hence do not supply it to retailers. With a complete understanding of her environment and needs, opportunities created by this niche market have well been served by her. Potential clients have been identified and hence providing a chance for Darmar to position herself well in the market.

According to article by Thilmany, 2008, there are great advantages of identifying and serving a niche market. This is because there are no competitions since businesses are not aware of the market hence the ability for you to continue satisfying the portion of the market and generate more profits. Most customers are accessible in the case of Darmar making it easy for her to capitalize in artifacts importation. This can make the niche market grow fast enough since retailers have access to the resources to run their businesses and assurance that their businesses will be sustained with the supply of the products that they need. Since the supply of artifacts to the small retailers is not owned by any one established vendor but Darmar only who organizes the supply of the artifacts as required by her customer it is easy for the business to grow fast.

According to Yim & Rok (2009), niche players understand their customers' needs and ability making it easy for them to satisfy them. They are also constantly engaged with customers providing them a chance to check on the required quality and their well-being. Identifying a niche market allows a business to develop and position itself in the market strongly and win the loyalty of the customers before other players get in the market. Therefore, niche markets are opportunities for growth which when well analyzed and research on the demands of the customers, capital required, accessibility of the customers and quality of products required can result to growth of a business.

References

Thilmany, D. (2008, January). *What are Niche Markets? What Advantages do They Offer?*

Retrieved from Colorado State University:

http://ag.arizona.edu/AREC/wemc/nichemarkets/01whatarenichemarkets.pdf

Wong-MingJi, D. J. (1999, May). *Defining and Developing Niche Markets: Strategic*

Opportunities for Caribbean Businesses. Retrieved from Bowling Green State

University: http://ufdcimages.uflib.ufl.edu/CA/00/40/02/13/00001/PDF.pdf

Yim, & Rok, H. (2009). *A Strategic Pathway to the Rapid-Growth of New Startups: Niche*

Marketing and Strategic Investment. Retrieved from Kyung Hee University:

http://sbaer.uca.edu/research/icsb/2009/paper1.pdf